WHAT ENGINEERS DO

Reagan Miller

HOW ENGINEERING AFFECTS OUR EVERYDAY LIVES

LIGHTBOX
openlightbox.com

LIGHTBOX

Go to **www.openlightbox.com** and enter this book's unique code.

ACCESS CODE

LBXY4379

Lightbox is an all-inclusive digital solution for the teaching and learning of curriculum topics in an original, groundbreaking way. Lightbox is based on National Curriculum Standards.

OPTIMIZED FOR

- ✓ TABLETS
- ✓ WHITEBOARDS
- ✓ COMPUTERS
- ✓ AND MUCH MORE!

STANDARD FEATURES OF LIGHTBOX

AUDIO High-quality narration using text-to-speech system

VIDEOS Embedded high-definition video clips

ACTIVITIES Printable PDFs that can be emailed and graded

WEBLINKS Curated links to external, child-safe resources

SLIDESHOWS Pictorial overviews of key concepts

INTERACTIVE MAPS Interactive maps and aerial satellite imagery

QUIZZES Ten multiple choice questions that are automatically graded and emailed for teacher assessment

KEY WORDS Matching key concepts to their definitions

VIDEOS

WEBLINKS

SLIDESHOWS

QUIZZES

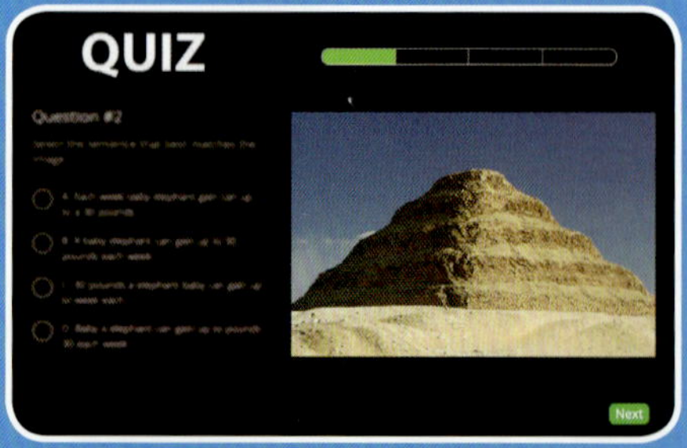

WHAT ENGINEERS DO

HOW ENGINEERING AFFECTS OUR EVERYDAY LIVES

Contents

What Is Engineering?

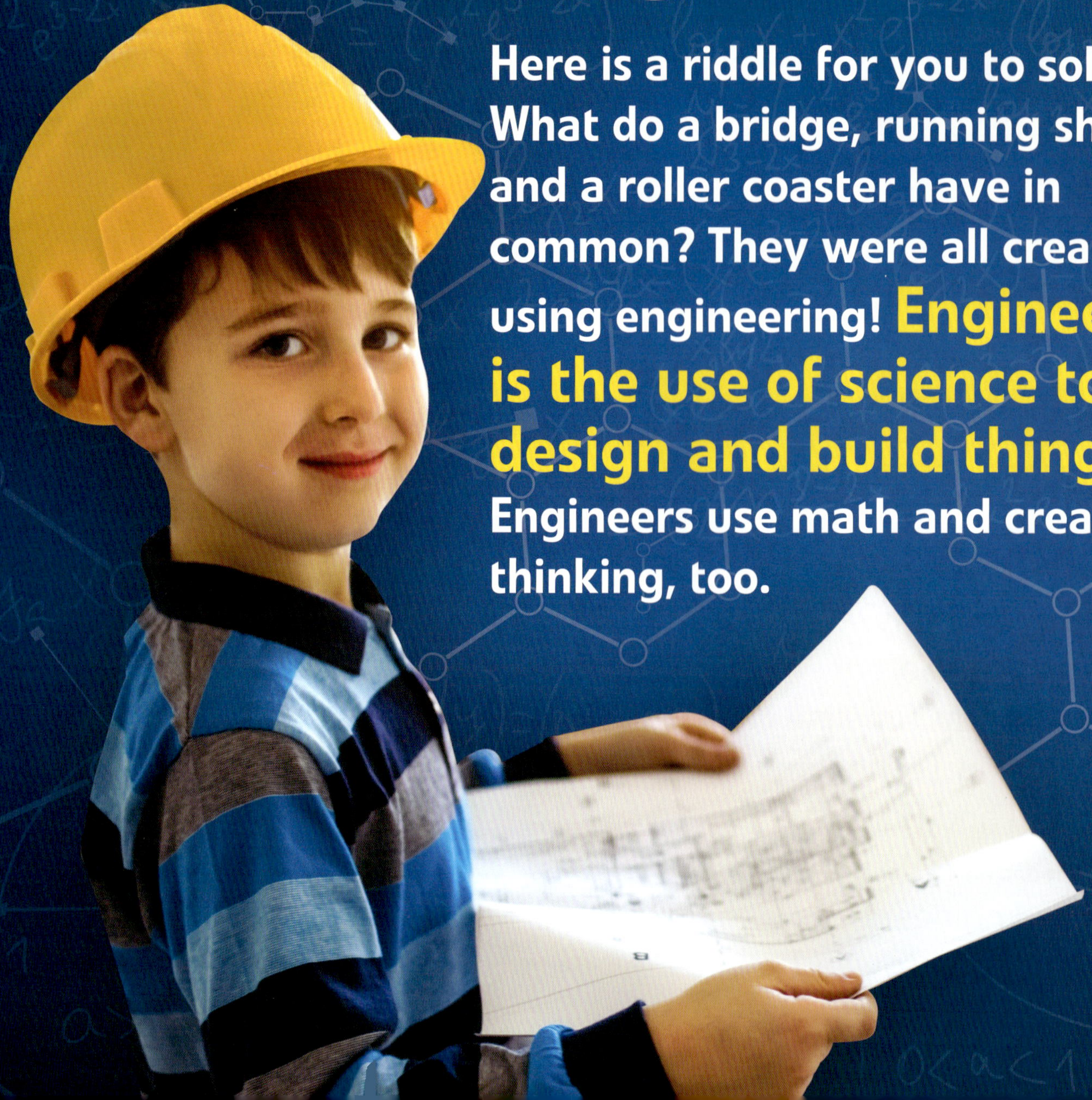

Here is a riddle for you to solve. What do a bridge, running shoes, and a roller coaster have in common? They were all created using engineering! **Engineering is the use of science to design and build things.** Engineers use math and creative thinking, too.

Think of some objects you use every day. Does your alarm clock wake you up in the morning? Do you carry a bag to school? Maybe you use a pencil to write.

Many things in our world were designed using engineering.

Engineers design things to make our lives safer and easier.

Most engineers go to **university** for at least **four years**.

What Is Technology?

The things that are designed by engineers are called technologies. **Technologies are created to solve a problem or meet a need.** A technology can be simple, such as a pencil. A pencil meets a person's need to write down information. Technology can also be complex. It may be made up of many different parts. A computer is a complex technology. It meets a person's need to find information quickly.

Technologies are designed by people. Things such as trees and rocks are natural. This means they come from nature. **Natural things are not technologies.** People do not design them.

Think like an engineer

Look at the pictures. Which pictures show technologies? Which pictures show things that are natural?

What Are Tools?

Tools are one kind of technology that engineers design. **They are objects that people use to make work easier and faster.** A shovel and a vacuum cleaner are both tools. People use shovels to dig holes. Vacuums help us clean carpets. Shovels and vacuums make work easier.

Engineers also design tools that help scientists discover new things. For example, a telescope is a tool. It makes far away objects look closer and larger. Telescopes help scientists discover and study objects in space, such as stars and planets.

Think like an engineer

What tools do people use to make work easier? Describe how these tools help in everyday life.

Health and Safety

Engineers design technologies that keep us safe and healthy. For example, they design tools and machines for doctors to use. These tools help doctors make us well when we are hurt or sick.

An x-ray machine is a technology. It is used in hospitals. The x-ray machine takes a picture called an x-ray. This picture shows the inside of the body. It even shows broken bones. An x-ray can help doctors learn where a person is injured.

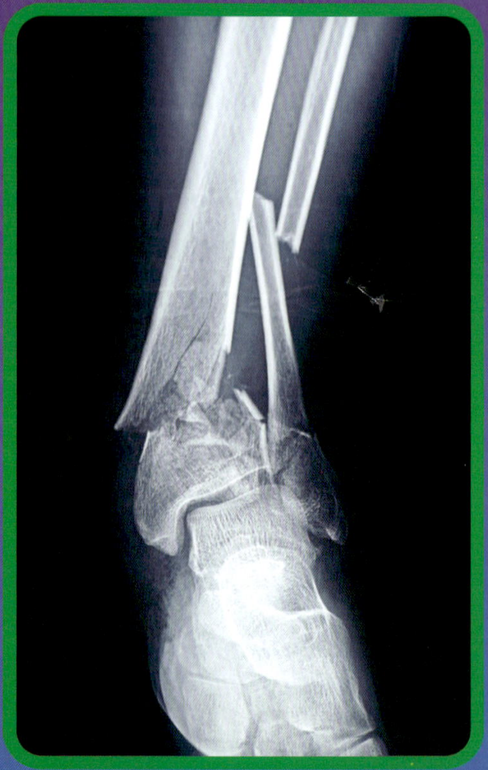

Think like an engineer

A traffic light is a technology that helps keep our roads safe. How do some other technologies help keep us safe and healthy?

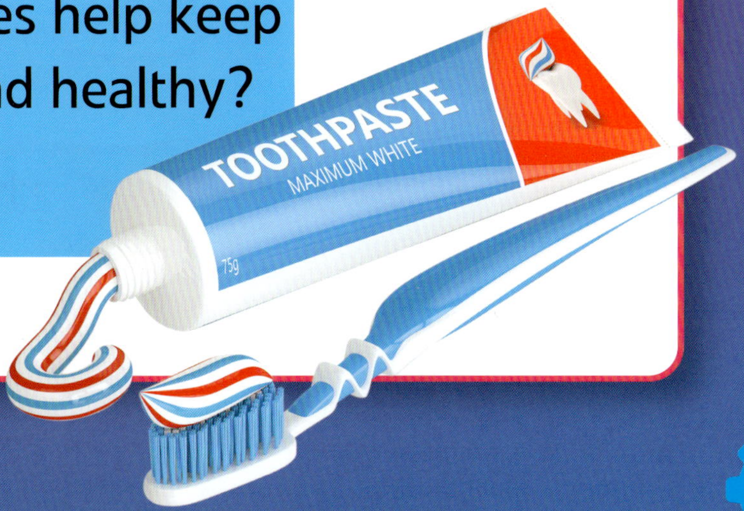

Technology Timeline

Technology is always changing. Engineers design new technologies. They also look for ways to make the technologies we have better.

1816

A man named Baron von Drais designs one of the first bicycles. It has two wooden wheels and no pedals. Riders have to use their feet to start and stop.

One example of this is the bicycle. **Engineers have changed bicycles over time.** Bicycles have become safer and more fun to ride.

1950

2000

1866

The Boneshaker bicycle is one of the first bicycles to have pedals. Pedals make the bicycle easier to ride, but its wooden wheels cause it to shake.

2020

Today, bicycle wheels have tires made of rubber. Rubber tires make riding smoother and more comfortable. Bicycles now also have hand brakes. The brakes make it easier to stop.

Improving Technology

Engineers study how things work. Then, they improve them. **Engineers believe there is always room for improvement.** Technologies can be improved in different ways. Engineers make things safer, faster, or easier to use.

Technology improves over time. The first televisions showed only black and white images. Engineers improved the technology. They created televisions that showed colored images. Remote controls were invented to change channels.

Helpful and Harmful

Technologies can be both helpful and harmful. We use technologies every day to solve problems. **Sometimes, however, using technology can cause problems.** For example, a car is a technology that people use to travel quickly from place to place. This makes it helpful. Cars also create pollution. This is harmful to the environment.

Technology can become harmful waste. Technology is always changing and improving. **What happens to old technology when new technology is created?** Many things get thrown away. They may end up in landfills. Computers and cell phones are made of materials that do not break down. They can cause harmful materials to leak into the land.

Every year, about **1 million seabirds** die from eating **plastic**.

Engineers Help Earth

Pollution is dangerous to our health. It harms Earth, too. Today, pollution is a major problem. Many engineers are trying to solve it. **Engineers work to design technologies that are less harmful to the environment.** For example, engineers design electric cars. Electric cars do not use gasoline. They create less pollution.

Engineers also find ways to recycle things. **To recycle means to make something new from something that has been used before.**

People throw away things such as newspapers and plastic bottles. These items can be recycled.

Many Engineers

There are many kinds of engineers. They work to solve different problems.

Some engineers work in offices and hospitals. Others may work in forests. Some even work in space! Aerospace engineers design aircraft and spacecraft. Civil engineers design buildings, bridges, tunnels, and roads.

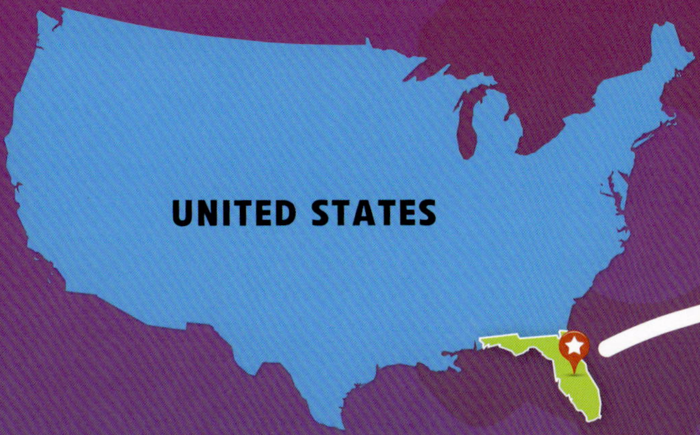

Are you a future engineer? **Engineers help make the world better, safer, and more fun.** Do you think you would like to be an engineer? Maybe someday you will design a technology that changes the world.

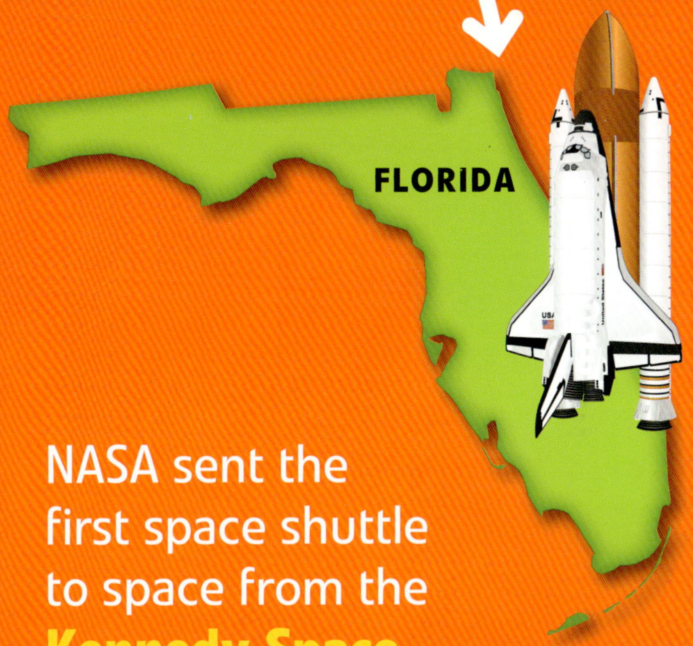

NASA sent the first space shuttle to space from the **Kennedy Space Center** in **Florida**.

ACTIVITY

Improve a Technology

Think of an object or tool that many people use. A bicycle, a cell phone, and a backpack are some examples. **How could you make it work better?** Could it do something it cannot do now? Come up with a way to improve the technology.

My Improved Bicycle

The Rain-or-Shine Rider

My bicycle is called the Rain-or-Shine Rider. It has an umbrella that clips on the seat. The umbrella keeps me dry when it is raining. It also gives me shade when it is sunny and hot.

1 Choose an object.

2 Think of ways you could improve the object. Make a list of ideas.

3 Choose your favorite idea. Draw a picture of your object or tool.

4 Describe the changes you made.

5 Explain how your changes make the object or tool better and more useful to people.

KEY WORDS

Research has shown that as much as 65 percent of all written material published in English is made up of 300 words. These 300 words cannot be taught using pictures or learned by sounding them out. They must be recognized by sight. This book contains 131 common sight words to help young readers improve their reading fluency and comprehension. This book also teaches young readers several important content words, such as proper nouns. These words are paired with pictures to aid in learning and improve understanding.

Page	Sight Words First Appearance
4	a, all, and, do, for, have, here, in, is, of, the, they, things, to, too, use, were, what, you
5	at, carry, day, does, every, four, go, lives, make, many, most, our, school, some, think, up, world, write, years, your
6	also, are, as, be, by, can, come, different, down, find, from, it, made, may, means, need, not, or, parts, people, such, that, them, this, trees
7	an, like, look, pictures, show, which
8	away, both, example, far, help, kind, new, one, study, us, work
9	how, life, these
10	even, keep, learn, takes, we, well, when
11	other
12	always, feet, first, has, man, no, start, stop, their, two, way
13	but, hand, its, more, now, over, time
14	then, there
15	change, only, white
16	car, place, sometimes
17	about, end, get, into, land, old
18	Earth
19	been, before, something
21	states, will, would

Page	Content Words First Appearance
4	bridge, engineering, engineers, math, riddle, roller coaster, science, shoes
5	alarm clock, bag, morning, objects, pencil, university
6	computer, information, nature, person, problem, rocks, technology
8	carpets, holes, planets, scientists, shovel, space, stars, telescope, tools, vacuum cleaner
10	body, bones, doctors, health, hospitals, machines, safety, x-ray
11	roads, traffic light
12	Baron von Drais, bicycles, pedals, wheels
13	Boneshaker, hand brakes, rubber tires
15	channels, images, remote controls, televisions
16	environment, pollution
17	cell phones, landfills, materials, seabirds, plastic, waste
18	electric cars, gasoline
19	bottles, items, newspapers
20	aerospace engineers, aircraft, bridges, buildings, civil engineers, forests, offices, spacecraft, tunnels
21	Florida, Kennedy Space Center, NASA, space shuttle, United States

Published by Smartbook Media Inc.
14 Penn Plaza, 9th Floor New York, NY 10122
Website: www.openlightbox.com

Library of Congress Control Number: 2020936986

ISBN 978-1-5105-5420-7 (hardcover)
ISBN 978-1-5105-5421-4 (multi-user eBook)

Printed in Guangzhou, China
1 2 3 4 5 6 7 8 9 0 24 23 22 21 20

052020
110819

Project Coordinator: Priyanka Das
Designer: Jean Faye Marie Rodriguez

The publisher acknowledges Getty Images, iStock, and Shutterstock as the primary image suppliers for this title.

First published by Crabtree Publishing Company in 2014.